I0521573

THE END HAS ALREADY PASSED...WHY ARE YOU STILL HERE?

What you need to know if your left behind after the rapture.

ROBERT JOHNSON

Copyright ©2022 Robert Johnson

All rights reserved. No part of this publication may be reproduced, distributed, or transmitted in any form or by any means, including photocopying, recording, or other electronic or mechanical methods, without the prior written permission of the publisher, except in the case of brief quotations embodied in critical reviews and other non-commercial uses permitted by copyright law. For permission requests, write to the publisher at the address below.

In accordance with the U.S. Copyright Act of 1976, the scanning, uploading, and electronic sharing of any part of this book without the permission of the publisher is unlawful piracy and theft of the author's intellectual property. Thank you for your support of the author's rights.

Permission: For information on getting permission for reprints and excerpts, contact:

Parenting Connections Publishing Group
2001 Timberloch Place, Suite 500
The Woodlands, TX 77380
info@parentingconnections.net

All scriptures are from the New King James Version of the Bi-ble unless otherwise indicated.
Scriptures taken from the Holy Bible, New International Ver-sion®, NIV®. Copyright © 1973, 1978, 1984, 2011 by Biblica, Inc.™ Used by permission of Zondervan. All rights reserved worldwide. www.zondervan.com The "NIV" and "New Inter-national Version" are trademarks registered in the United States Patent and Trade-mark Office by Biblica, Inc.®

ISBN: 979-8-9866295-6-8 (paperback)
ISBN: 979-8-9866295-7-5 (eBook)
ISBN : 9798362429089 (KDP)

THE END HAS ALREADY PAST...WHY ARE YOU STILL HERE?

Over my many years on earth, I have been very blessed by God with many spiritual dreams and visions. However, I found that most of these dreams were to take place after the rapture of the church. Following that knowledge, at church one day, all the pieces started to fit together. All of the spiritual dreams and visions, along with the title of this book, suddenly came alive.

This book is for you if you are still here after the church's rapture.

Salvation does not end with the rapture of the church. If you are still here post-rapture, take inventory of your life, see what went wrong and why

1

you were left behind. The hidden things in your life that you thought God had overlooked or would never see must have caught up with you. Don't hold yourself back any longer. Turn it over to God, and sincerely ask for His forgiveness through Jesus Christ, who laid down his life for all people, even you. However, you have to do your part.

There comes a time in every man's life when we ask ourselves - what am I here for? What is my purpose here on earth? Well, you were put here for a purpose. There must have been times when people or situations have spoken to you about accepting Jesus Christ as your Lord and Savior. You must have answered in the positive or negative, which is why you are here.

If your answer was 'yes,' eternity is yours to spend in Heaven with Jesus Christ, God the Father, and the Holy Spirit, who is the real author of this book. But if your answer was "no" to accepting the Lord Jesus Christ, who suffered and died for you, I would strongly encourage you to spend $15 to purchase and read the book by Mary K Baxter, titled 'The Divine Revelation of Hell.' Be strongly aware that this book is going to take you to hell…..the real honest-to-goodness hell. The author, with the Lord Jesus Christ, spent 30 nights in hell for her to write this must-read book to keep you out of hell. Hell or Heaven, you are going to spend eternity in one of these two places. It is your choice to decide which.

Allow me to explain eternity to you. If you take just one grain of sand, walk it to the moon, and then back to the earth, repeating the process until there are no more grains of sand left on the earth. Even when you also do that to the other eight planets, eternity will only just have begun.

How, then, do I accept the Lord Jesus Christ? What is salvation? What is repentance? All of these begin with your mindset and heart.

This is a wake-up call. It starts with self-examining yourself and your physical and spiritual life. Ask for help from the Holy Spirit to open your spiritual eyes and mind, as you cannot do it your-self because it is a supernatural act. Examine your life, particularly in the search for the wrong you have done in your lifetime and what you are doing now that drives you away from God. Search your mind and heart to see if you are sorry; it's called repentance.

You must be genuinely remorseful and be willing to change your way of life for good. God looks at the heart and knows whether you mean it or not. So, ask the Holy Spirit to condition your mind and heart. How long it takes you to do this is entirely up to you, but you will be delighted when you do. You will have a very strong desire to tell everyone about it.

Right now, in your privacy, bow your head, and in all humbleness, talk to Jesus about your sins and wrongdoing. He is eager to hear from you. Very humbly and meekly, ask Jesus to forgive you of your sins and to come into your life, changing you in his favor to enable you to be a member of the family of God.

No pressure, but I would love to remind you to look at what is going on in the world today. Russia, China, North Korea, Iran, and other countries want to destroy the United States. And this is possible with nuclear weapons.

I have been studying the Bible since March 1972, and I know what the Bible says and how close we are to the end of the world. We are dangerously close to being wiped out, just as Ukraine has been. Everyone has nuclear weapons, and they all hate America.

What does the rapture of the church imply? The word 'rapture' is not found in the Bible; the same goes for the word 'Bible,' but I'm reading one. God's power is great, beyond measure and understanding. Let's check out first Corinthians 15: 51 and 52:

"Behold I show you a mystery: we shall not all sleep, but we shall all be changed in a moment... in the blinking of the eye (11/100th of a second) at the last trump......."

The Bible calls it the great catching away. God's people will be caught up to Heaven in one blink of an eye, so get yourself ready! This is the rapture of the church.

The spiritual dreams and visions written in this book are some that the Lord has blessed me with over the past 50 years since I was saved. These will all take place after the church's rapture in and on the earth. Pay close attention to what I am going to write to you.

MARCH 8, 1972

I was in a bar with friends in Long Beach, CA, where I lived at the time, and the church was in Los Angeles, CA. My friends and I were all pumped up and excited about a spiritual event called a revival that would take place later that evening. I was 100% solid Catholic, so I thought it would be fun, coupled with the fact that I was with all my friends. When we got to the church, the excitement of the presence of the Holy Spirit was overwhelming for us.

After the message by the pastor, Lee Carlton, there was an altar call. At first, I was afraid to go up to the front of the church, but when I saw so many people doing that, I followed suit. When I did, I felt a very warm feeling inside of me, and I knew it was the Holy Spirit. For three days, I felt like I was floating on air. I wanted to tell everyone about this supernatural experience that happened to me, and I did.

About six weeks after my encounter in that church, I started having spiritual dreams and visions. I did not know what to do with them at the time, so I wrote them down alongside the dates and times. It's going to be really bad, and I will be sharing some of them with you in this book.

More than 50 years have passed since I received these spiritual dreams and visions, and I only recently discovered they are to take place after the rapture of the church. On May 7, 2022, the Holy Spirit started bringing to my notice this book. Oh! There is so much information that I have about what will happen after the church's rapture when God takes his people home to Heaven. Are you coming? Look around you and see what is happening in countries in the world. Do not wait much longer to accept the Lord Jesus Christ as your Savior. He died to save you from your sins.

God waited so many years after giving me these visions and spiritual dreams to write this book and show you the devastation that is coming on the earth. Habakkuk Chapter 2: Verses 1,2 and 3:

"I will stand upon my watch and set me upon the tower and watch to see what He will say unto me and what I shall answer when I am reproved. And the Lord answered me, and said, write the vision and make it plain on tables that he may run in great fear that he that readeth it. For the vision is yet for an appointed time, and at the end, it shall speak and not lie though it tarry, wait for it because it will surely come. It will not tarry. It will not delay."

What I am about sharing with you is going to send shockwaves to all who read these proceeding pages. Will you be here to live through all this?

First of all, let's take a look at Zachariah 14:12. If you do not have a Bible, this is what it says:

"and this shall be the plague wherewith the Lord will smite all the people....... their flesh shall consume away while they stand up on their feet and their eyes shall consume away in their eye sockets, and their tongue shall consume away in their mouth all before they hit the ground."

This part of the scripture talks about nuclear bombs, which are knocking on your door since so many nations now have them.

September 19, 2011

All the stores like Walmart and Target, small and big stores alike, will all be changed and take on a whole new look. The lights inside the stores will be dimmed down to only about 30% to gain mind and body control over you. This will all happen after the rapture of the church. All the people will live only in restraining camps, but I will talk about this a little later.

The big stores like Walmart and Target will be redesigned into eight or ten sections, carrying only the bare necessities. From these restraining camps where everyone will live, a bus will convey all the people to and from the stores. These buses will take you to the door you are appointed to go in. The eight or ten sections of the store will have only necessities and nothing more, unlike what they look like today. It will all be gone except for what you need. You won't have very much time to get what you need and will be forced to stay in your own section of the store.

A store guard will stand at the end of every counter, watching you and what you buy. When the time is up, everyone in his own section of the store goes to the end of the aisle to pay for what they have purchased by displaying the 666 mark on their right hand, while those with the 666 mark on their forehead will be the people in authority. The seats on the buses will all be numbered; thus, you must sit in your seat when traveling to the store and back to your restraining camp. Everyone is programmed to sit quietly in their own seat until the end of the ride.

DECEMBER 18, 2011

Our present government has the ability to reduce the human body back into molecules, as in the old Star Trek movies, some 50 or more years ago. This is what these restraining camps are set up for all around the country.

There are also different kinds of computer chips present, implanted in people who go into restraining camps. The chips take away the people's fight and desire, turning them into zombies. The old will be the first because they are the most dependent on the government for financial support. The financial drain on the government will be over, and the world governments will use this money for military armament escalation. The computer chip implants going into the bodies of the military and police will turn them into fighting machines.

If you can envision any of this in your mind, this vision is talking to you. All medical attention and medicine will be denied to older adults because they will not be able to pay for these services. When people die for one reason or the other, their blood is removed and re-processed by medical practitioners. It is used to aid militants who have been injured in this worldwide war spoken of in the Book of Revelation and other parts of the Bible.

The tracking devices from our government, which are being used against you, are all around, and you are being watched all around the clock. These devices can be found in your phone, television, computer, and all other electrical devices you use, and also in your implants. This information will go back to the government to be used as leverage against you for one reason or the other.

In addition to all these, the store cash registers have a second roll of register tape inside of them.

One is your copy of the purchases you have, and the other register tape inside the cash register lists all your purchases in the store. However, this copy goes to the government for the store's taxes. This tape is also a reading of what you like, and the government will withhold these items from you at their will.

The Holy Spirit has expanded the measure of my mind again today. This must be very important to God to bring this up a second time for you. As I wrote earlier in this book, all the people that are left behind and did not make it into Heaven when the Lord called his church in the rapture (or this supernatural catching away), here it is again for the second time: For all those who are left behind, you are all going to have your bodies inserted with a computer chip, and a programming device whether willing or not. 'human robots' is the term I am getting from the Lord. There will be no resistance from the people who have this chip inserted in them.

JULY 28, 2011

The first order of business is to program all the individuals of the military and law enforcement from the top tier of government down to the local townships and all the Great American cities.

I find that repetition is the best teacher. God has a reason for me to explain this in greater detail to you.

Here's how millions of people fit into all of this. All people will be taken to these restraining camps to live and die. And again, I say, you're going to join them if you are left behind, says God. Enormous amounts of blood will be shipped to the Middle East as the Book of Revelation Chapter 14: 20 is fulfilled. The best way is to see for yourself and read Ezekiel Chapters 38 and 39.

You will see the bombs and rockets coming low over your neighborhood skies. Read Daniel Chapters 7, 8, 9, and all the books of Daniel if you can. The end of Daniel Chapter 12 talks about Daniel closing the book and its prophecies until the end, when they will be fulfilled. This information I am writing to you came to me several years ago. Like Daniel, it wasn't the time for this information to be written down in this book, as it came to me all these years later through the moving of the Holy Spirit. As I continue in these following pages, I am sharing the move of God in Daniel's writings and also in my writings to show you how God works with his Word.

OCTOBER 5, 2011

HD- high definition or hidden device? It is most likely a camera or some sort of tracking device to keep you under surveillance during the tribulation. There will also be hidden devices in your vehicle. Actually, tracking devices are already in them, and your every move will be watched. As I said, the HD code is not for you. It is a government code to keep track of you, watching what you do in your home, in front of your television set and computer, and where you travel. So, be very careful what you do in front of them.

That HD device code means nothing to us as it is for the government's use only. It monitors the TV programs you watch and the search engines you use on your computer. This information is sent to a database for later use against you, resulting in them cutting off all the TV programs you like to watch until you conform to receive the mark of the beast, 666. They will also cut off food supplies that you like, perhaps all food supplies.

True believers, keep your eyes on the eastern skies. Lift your heads; your redemption is drawing near.

Try to expand the measure of your understanding of what I'm telling you. Over the years of our lifetime, we have heard the term in situations where people tell us the sky is falling. Well, folks, it is, and it is happening now. Look at the world situation and what is happening right now. Trust me. You don't want to be a part of all that is coming.

Find a quiet place to be alone and talk to the Lord, telling him you know you are a sinner. Ask him to forgive you and for Jesus to come into your heart. Stop doing the things you know that are wrong. Jesus loves you and will forgive you.

Newsflash! Newsflash! Newsflash!! The television and radio news media will never broadcast the disappearance of all these millions of people who suddenly vanish off the earth. The news media are all very aware of what happened in the vast disappearance and will not tell you the truth. They will, instead, tell you it was an outer space experience. The news media has been brainwashing you for several years now with fake news, and they are very good at it.

The news media will be one of the most significant tools used by the Antichrist movement. In any way they can, they will beat you until you don't know the truth from their lies. You are the enemy of the government, and the news media will not let you go until you give up. But not all is lost on television. Today, Newsmax will give you the truth, but after the rapture, they may be gone and off the air.

NOVEMBER 25, 2011

The biggest and most terrifying secret of all nations is overpopulation. It is hidden from the world because its knowledge will cause widespread panic, and millions of people will kill each other. A thousand bodies will need to be taken care of daily, with everyone's life on the line. Everyone on earth will be a target of being killed.

All guns and ammunition will be removed from the possession of all individuals, save the government, military, and police force, who will all have weapons, and the hollow point bullet will become their favorite. This is how their thinking process goes.

Germ agencies will be released into the air but not in a gas form like when they killed millions of people in World War One from 1914 to 1918. This germ agency being released will calm people into submission, as one day, a hush will fall in the footsteps of us all. We will echo down the hall and disappear.

Drones and heat sensors are now perfected to the point that they can track down people from a great distance. Your government will have you tracked down and killed in a matter of days should you decide not to accept the mark of the beast (666).

People who have millions of dollars are constructing buildings underground, thinking they can hide from the devastation that's coming on the earth. However, the heat-seeking drones will find you wherever you are, underground or on the mountaintop, as the Bible prophecy must be fulfilled in both the Old and New Testaments. These drones will fly over the whole earth, loaded with machine guns and heat sensors.

These infrared heat sensors will also be on low-flying helicopters, vehicles, and drones. This prophecy comes into reality in the seven-year tribulation, where people will be running quickly, frantically searching for a hiding place far out into the countryside, as they will be hunted down for refusing to accept the mark of the beast (666). But your hiding place will be exposed by helicopters and drones.

On the ground, thousands of people will be transported to these restraining camps, never to be heard from again. No one will be in hiding for very long. Very powerful lasers will burn their way through everything, man-made or not.

You will have a decision to make, thinking of if you want it In your right or left hand. But there's another too - Is it to go through all of this and then go into hell for taking the mark of the beast (666), or accept the Lord Jesus Christ as your Savior now and live eternally in Heaven? The choice is yours.

One more thing about the Christians going to Heaven is that we will immediately be standing face to face with our Lord, Savior, and Redeemer, Jesus Christ, and the Books will be opened. There will be two Books with all the things we have done here on earth, both good and bad. Everything! They will all be stacked, one on top of another, of all you have done. Then, the Holy Ghost and fire will come down from the top over all your life's work, good and bad, until He reaches the bottom. The bad things will be burned up in the fire, the good things that come through the fire will be everlasting to the glory of God, and the Lord will say to you, "Enter into my rest, thou good and faithful servant."

Are you not ever so hungry for the Lord Jesus Christ to say this to you? He can if you will say "yes" and accept him as the Lord and Savior of your life.

DECEMBER 28, 2011

As I was getting out of bed at about 7:15 AM, the Holy Spirit said to me, "You haven't seen anything yet."

1-1-2012 "The judgment of thy works is very near at hand and will come suddenly. Strive always to do good and always be in obedience", thus sayeth the Lord.

1-2-2012 The Holy Spirit urged me to read Revelation Chapter 17:18. I discovered that Mystery Babylon the Great, spoken thereof, is the United States of America. Read

Revelation Chapters 17 and 18, taking note of how this country fits into these two Chapters.

The big question is this; is the United States hidden in Bible prophecy? Yes! America is in the Bible prophecy, but you must hunt and search the scriptures for it, especially in the Book of Revelation. The Holy Spirit will lead you if you ask Him; you will seek and find Him if you want this with all your mind and heart. Simply ask.

Here is some food for thought. Life is a fast-moving train. Looking at 80 years of age on the horizon of my life, I see myself on a train moving very fast. Looking out the windows of this train of life, I see nothing but a blur of colors rushing me to my getting-off place, which is death. But it did not start off like this in the beginning, up until it is discovered that there is no ending to this train of life. Everyone is on this train, and it makes frequent stops to life's end. It starts out very slow at the beginning but picks up speed as our years go rolling by.

Have you ever noticed that in the three years of Jesus Christ's ministry, only one time, he spoke plainly so that all people could understand him (Matthew Chapter 5, the Sermon on the Mount)? All the rest of the words of his three-year ministry he spoke only in parables.

You who are reading this book need to know about evil forces. I do not know how many millions or billions of years ago there was a rebellion in Heaven when Satan was the most beautiful creation of all God's spiritual beings. We read it in Isaiah Chapter 14: 12 - 15. I'll write it all down if you don't have a Bible.

"How thou art fell from Heaven O' Lucifer (the devil), son of the morning! How art thou cut down to the ground? For thou hast said in thine heart, I will ascend into Heaven. I will exalt my throne above the

stars of God. I will sit and ascend above the heights of the clouds. I will be like the most high God. Yet thou shall be brought down to hell to the sides of the pit.

Thou hast been in Eden, the garden of God. Every precious stone was thy covering. Twelve stones, tablets, and pipes the day thou was created. Thou was the anointed cherub that covereth, and I, God, have set these so. Thou was upon the holy mountain of God. Thou has walked up and down in the midst of the precious stones of fire; thou was perfect in all thy ways from the day thou was created till iniquity was found in thee. Thine heart was lifted up because of thy beauty. Thou hast corrupted thy wisdom by reason of thy brightness. I will cast thee to the ground......."

Pray for your spiritual understanding and for your ears and eyes to be unplugged. Try to look ahead as to what is coming in our country. It may

not look like anything will happen today, but be-
ware, it is on its way.

MARCH 10, 2021

The Holy Spirit was communicating today with my spirit. All the banks in this country are going to collapse, not reopening, and your money will become worthless. This country has many enemies that have perfected the counterfeiting of currency and will flood the world markets with counterfeit American currency.

Take serious note of the money you have in the banks and redistribute as you see fit for future use. This warning from the Holy Spirit is for you now, today. Be wise and listen to his words. Some money, but not very much, as you may want to leave it in the bank. But have plenty of cash on hand and don't get caught short.

MAY 30, 2022

On Newsmax television, there is a worldwide food shortage coming in about ten weeks. You may consider investing in dehydrated or freeze-dried food sold in five-gallon containers, which can be stored for up to 25 years in air-conditioned or heated rooms.

Theft will be rampant, as well as murder and killing, which will also be on the agenda.

Prepare yourselves as best you can, as prices for everything will continue to skyrocket out of sight, with Gas prices heading the list. A wise move is to buy a locked gas cap for your vehicles, just as I did about 20 years ago.

Keep the Lord first in all you do and all you say, and pray continuously. Remember, He is still in charge and knows everything that is going on in your life and the world. Now would be the perfect time to turn your life over to the Lord, seek his forgiveness, and be saved.

The evil forces of the rebellion are the fallen angels. Who are they, and why are they after my family and me?

We have only some information about what happened concerning these fallen angels and why they hate us so much. I'll share my understanding with you. It started in the garden with Adam and Eve, sin and disobedience as the main culprits. You all know the story of Adam and Eve. God is serious about sin, and He's not playing around.

We inherited sin at birth from Adam and Eve's disobedience in the garden of Eden when they ate the forbidden fruit. Satan overpowered Eve, and Adam fell victim also. The devil, Satan, hates us and the human race. He has played a significant part in the ongoing sin in our lives after we were born. For over 6000 years, the Jewish people were God's chosen people and still are today. They are the guardians of the Ten Commandments and the Laws of the Old Testament, as well as the prophecies, were spoken by the prophets in both the Old and New Testaments. For Satan to rise above God, in his feeble mind of error, he would have to have put an end to the Jesus movement from the beginning, and that never happened. Christianity is still alive and well. Satan hates all of us who are connected to God in any way.

The Holocaust of 1933-1945 was and is very real. Read Ezekiel Chapter 37 and see the power of God in the valley of dry bones. To every believer in the Lord Jesus Christ, Satan and all his evil forces are constantly tempting us, causing us grief or harm, and doing all they can to get us to turn away from God. Read the Book of Job in the Old Testament.

Don't worry about Satan and all his evil forces for those who are not saved by the blood of the Lord Jesus Christ and are not interested in his salvation plan. Go ahead and continue to live in sin and immorality. Keep your mindset, "If it feels good, do it." Continue in your lives of lies, hatred, sin, and all your wild ways. Satan is not after you and will not disrupt your life. He already has you, as you are his, and hell is your destination.

In the following pages, I would like to share with you a few things that have taken place in my life, which were brought on by the evil forces of Satan. Remember, good and evil spirits are spirits but will only reveal themselves to you if they wish to. Evil forces are real!

MARCH 4, 2012

They shouted, "There he is! Get him! Don't let him get away!" As I slept between a late night on Sunday, March 4, and early Monday, March 5, the most frightening, terrifying, and nightmarish vision came upon me. It startled me so much that I will never forget it as long as I live. These very evil demons came upon me, about 10 or 12 in number, and I was paralyzed by them. I was in great fear and in a trance for no less than two hours. Their hatred towards me as they hovered over and in front of me is beyond the description by words in the human vocabulary. The evil beings' power over me was so great that they expounded no effort to subdue me. I remained in this shocking terror as their prisoner for what seemed to be a lifetime. I felt as though they wanted to torture me into a slow and painful death. The hatred in their eyes and on their faces is what I remember most since they all were only inches away from me.

As I woke up the following day, March 5, 2012, I found myself very sick and badly shaken up for most of the day. I called my pastor but could not put this experience into words. I finally did talk to the pastor and followed his direct instructions, anointing all the walls and doors of my house with holy oil. In praying over these doors and walls, the Holy Spirit reminded me that the Holy oil in itself is a powerful force in repelling and preventing even the greatest evil force from entering my place or property.

Many people poured heavy prayers out over the doors, walls, and property. That same day, I started researching many books to see what I could find out about my spiritual warfare, evil spirits, and other people's experiences with evil spirits that were written down. I found none, not even one.

MARCH 14, 2012

Far away from the location mentioned above and the earlier pages of evil forces, I was now living in a new location, unlike the location of the one I shared with you previously. I was lying in my bed asleep when I once again saw the same evil demons I had seen several nights before.

This night vision put me back at Lakewood Church, where I was a member for several years. I was in the last row of the third balcony to the far right. All of the lights were off, and it was pitch black, with only the church stage lit up with very bright lights. I was far away from the stage and all its bright lights. On the stage, about twelve evil forces were doing some kind of dance ritual that went on for several long minutes on the stage while all the stage lights were on. Suddenly, the lights went off, and the building was thrown into darkness.

I was down between the seats hiding and could sense very strongly the evil forces moving through the sanctuary's aisles, searching for me. As terrified as I was, I crouched down even more between the seats hoping not to be detected.

I could feel the evil forces getting closer and closer to me, as if they knew exactly where I was. Suddenly, they were all nearly on top of me in my hiding place. Then, all of the bright lights came on over the auditorium, and once again, I saw on their faces all the hate and evil directed at me as it was in the previous vision. Then I woke up, aware that evil forces exist and that they do not like any of us. Read 'A Divine Revelation of Hell' by Mary K. Baxter.

Good spiritual things have also happened to me in my lifetime, as I am very blessed by God. I'll share one or two of these good spiritual things that have taken place in my life, but that's all because the focus is not on me. It's about you, your decision, and where you want to spend eternity, with or without Jesus Christ in your life.

NOVEMBER 28, 2011

I was asleep in my bed, and a very blessed and profound spiritual dream came to me. I was walking down the middle of a street with no cars, trucks, or traffic anywhere in sight. This street was very dark and long, with an open field on one side, thick bushes on the other, and no homes or buildings. Coming towards me, as I faced east, was a shadowy figure of what looked like a man. As he walked closer to me, I saw that he was carrying a large bag on his shoulder. This huge bag was the size we had all seen, like a big Santa Claus bag full of toys. That's how big this bag was.

As he got closer to me, I could see that this bag was not filled with toys. He had a big smile on his face and came near me, then threw the bag high into the air over me. The bag came open in mid-air, and all the bag's contents showered down over me. Out of the bag came the purest gold Nuggets I have ever seen. This huge bag was full of them, and they were all around me.

I took the bag the gold was in, filling it with the gold Nuggets. I filled the bag so full of gold that not even one more nugget would fit inside. But still, so much gold was still left on the ground all around me. I picked up my large bag of gold and put it on my shoulder, sorely distressed at having to leave so much gold on the ground behind me as I moved on with my large bag of gold.

Up ahead, about 30 or 40 feet, I saw again this exact shadowy figure of a man, even the same man, and he again had a very large bag on his shoulder as he walked down the street. I then woke up from my spiritual dream.

I will share only one more spiritual dream out of the many I have had in these past 50 years. I am taking the time to share these with you to prove to you that God is real, and so are Satan and his evil forces.

One more, here it is. Pay attention! Jesus may be talking to you right now. I'm not writing this for myself but for you. I am trying to get this across to you, who are last and on your way to hell. This is serious business, folks, and you are running out of time! Look what is taking place in the world today! This is your wake-up call. Don't miss it!

I worked at Dow Chemical on Battleground Road for ten-plus years. This plant is in Deer Park, TX. In this spiritual dream, I was working nights. As I entered gate 9 to go to my work location, I suddenly found myself in a carnival. The surrounding colors were very brilliant and alive. A warm feeling came over me as I was submerged in this bright light.

The music was so beautiful that I could not begin to put it into words. It was absolutely indescribable. It was like hundreds of beautiful chimes perfectly in tune with the songs being sung. The range of these chimes and songs was in perfect accord, one with another. It was soprano, Alto, tenor, and baritone in perfect harmony. I just wanted to sit and listen to the music for all eternity. The kind of music that they play and sing in Heaven is the same music that is played and sung here on earth. And the vision ended.

In conclusion, to you who are on the "yes" or "no" fence in accepting the Lord Jesus Christ as your Savior and Redeemer, I can only say that I have done the very best I can to bring you the truth of Heaven and hell in this book.

Wisdom is highly valued by God. Make the wise decision and make Heaven your home.

Hope to see you there,
Robert Johnson

www.ingramcontent.com/pod-product-compliance
Lightning Source LLC
Chambersburg PA
CBHW020343130626
46549CB00003B/1272